WONDERFUL

1

Fabric
Quilts

Kay Nickols

American Quilter's Society
P. O. Box 3290 • Paducah, KY 42002-3290
www.AmericanQuilter.com

Located in Paducah, Kentucky, the American Quilter's Society (AQS) is dedicated to promoting the accomplishments of today's quilters. Through its publications and events, AQS strives to honor today's quilt-makers and their work and to inspire future creativity and innovation in quiltmaking.

EDITOR: LINDA BAXTER LASCO
GRAPHIC DESIGN: ELAINE WILSON
COVER DESIGN: MICHAEL BUCKINGHAM
PHOTOGRAPHY: CHARLES R. LYNCH

Library of Congress Cataloging-in-Publication Data

Nickols, Kay.
Wonderful 1-fabric quilts / by Kay Nickols.
 p. cm.
 Summary: "Quiltmaking design process and construction method using one fabric. Technique requires no special tools. Step-by-step instructions illustrate process for easily constructed quilts"--Provided by publisher.
 ISBN 978-1-57432-936-0
 1. Patchwork--Patterns. 2. Quilting--Patterns. 3. Kaleidoscope quilts. I. Title. II. Title: Wonderful one-fabric quilts.
 TT835.N4945 2007
 746.46'041--dc22

        2007027475

Additional copies of this book may be ordered from the American Quilter's Society, PO Box 3290, Paducah, KY 42002-3290, or online at www.AmericanQuilter.com. For phone orders only 800-626-5420. For all other inquiries, call 270-898-7903.

Proudly printed and bound in the United States of America

Dedication

To the Almighty for showing me a new way to quilt and to Rollie for his patience with my crazy hours of creativity.

To my students who encouraged me to write about one-fabric quilts.

To all of the quilters who have yet to try this great new process. Make many quilts and glow in your creativity.

Acknowledgments

This book would not have come about if it was not for a challenge set forth by my friend Sherry Epple.

Sincere thanks to Linda Baxter Lasco and Nicole Chambers for being so patient with a first-time author, and to Elaine Wilson, Charles R. Lynch, and Michael Buckingham at AQS.

I humbly thank the quilters who have been kind enough to share their quilts and quilting with me. They are Kerrie Nell Addis, Becky Arambula, Sue Cole, Alecia Debello, Mary Dharamraj, Jan Gagliano, Vicky Hartig, Pam Henrys, Cindy Hogan, Robyn House, Dorothy Jones, Jean Kaufmann, Chris McEnhill, Peg Mettler, Dorothy Mills, Louise Mueller, Kim Nickols, Helen Novak, Cyndi Pearson, Helen Prine, John Putnam, Joyce Putnam PhD, Amy Reed, Marian Reed, David Showerman, Sharon Showerman, Pam Smolek, Pat Stinson, Florence Vogt, and Stella Wilcox.

A special thanks to the following groups and quilt shops without whom these one-of-a-kind quilts would not have been created:

Around the Block Quilt Shop, Portland, Michigan
Capitol City Quilt Guild, Lansing, Michigan
Custom Quilts and Sewing, Haslett, Michigan
Foster Friday Group, Lansing, Michigan
Lansing Area Patchers, Lansing, Michigan
Lunch Bunch, Lansing, Michigan
Mary's Quilts and Things, Swartz Creek, Michigan
Material Girls, Lansing, Michigan
Pedal Pushers, Lansing, Michigan
Saginaw Piecemakers Quilt Guild, Saginaw, Michigan
Shiawassee Quilters, Owosso, Michigan

Preface

I love fabrics that are designed using a striped motif. These beautiful fabrics have curved- or straight-line stripes and are mixed with lovely florals and novelty characters. Many times these fabrics are overlooked for quiltmaking because they are hard to coordinate with other fabrics or because the stripes may be filled with too many elements that look difficult to use.

I love to make unique quilts and I love the freedom of working without a pattern. When I finally figured out a way to use stripes without having to follow a pattern, I wanted to share the process.

My one-fabric process provides more time for quilters to make more quilts. Time is saved in several ways. Cutting is quick and efficient. You can eliminate the time it takes to shop for special tools or for coordinating fabrics. You don't have to shop again when you discover you are half a yard short of a particular fabric needed to finish a quilt.

The quilters who have tried this new process have been so pleased with the beautiful and quick results that they have made many quilts this way. They have found that using just one fabric for the whole top gives surprising and fun results.

Shopping for one beautiful striped fabric and making it work for the whole quilt top is a delightful challenge. As you work with this process, basic quilt designs progress to more intricate placement ideas, letting you create unique quilts that make the soul sing.

There is a great variety of ideas shown in quilts constructed by my students and me. Make the fabric work for you. Join in the pleasure of making a surprise quilt from one fabric. You will have a great time designing your own quilts.

Contents

Shopping for a One-Fabric Quilt

Shopping is an exciting part of the one-fabric process. Look for stripes with interest, contrast, color, and a variety of scale. You'll find florals, novelty prints, geometric designs mixed with animals, and more. Stripes can run horizontally or vertically. The choices are unlimited.

For the one-fabric quilt, look for the very best quality fabric to get the most reliable cuts. It is disappointing to begin measuring and find that the design is misprinted on the fabric. Such fabrics make uniform cuts difficult or impossible.

How Much Fabric?

A wallhanging-size quilt top can be made from four yards of fabric. Six yards of fabric will make a lap-size top. Six to eight yards of fabric will make a queen-size top if random cuts are made. Fussy cuts will require more fabric (see Where to Cut, page 16).

Vertical Print Stripes

The vertical print stripes are often called wallpaper prints. Stripes and floral combinations are common. Sometimes there are birds or animals in the print.

The floral or print part of the design is often wider than the geometric, striped design. These fabrics can produce a quilt with a soft, romantic, Victorian look (figure 1).

Figure 1. Two- and three-striped design wallpaper prints

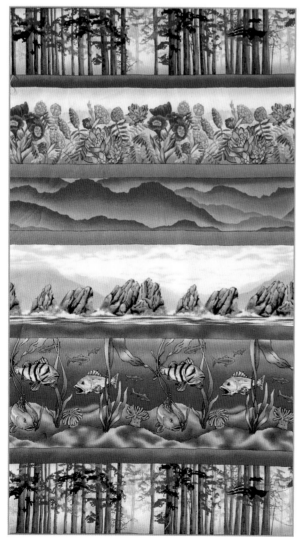

Figure 2. Horizontal novelty prints

> The repeat of the design dictates the finished size of your one-fabric blocks. The larger the repeat, the larger the squares you can cut, and the bigger the blocks you can make.

Horizontal Print Stripes

Fantastic stripes can be found in the novelty designs often located in the juvenile print sections of quilt shops. They are also found among decorator prints. These usually have a great variety of elements in the design.

Novelty and earth element design fabrics generally run horizontally but they can be found in vertical stripes as well (figure 2).

Sometimes there are so many stripes in the print that there are elements you won't want to use. There may be a color or motif that detracts from the more desirable parts of the print. You can simply eliminate the part of the fabric that you don't like when you make your block cuts.

Fabrics to Avoid

Stripes in prints that have the same value do not work as well as ones with light, medium, and dark values in the design (figure 3). High contrast in the stripes offers more options for surprising results.

Fabrics with a lot of negative space (more background than design) do not provide enough detail to create interesting designs (figure 4).

Prints that do not have a pronounced linear element should be avoided as they do not provide enough variety of design, but curvy stripes are OK (figure 5).

Busy stripes of like elements should not be used, as the end result is not very interesting (figure 6).

Figure 3. Stripes with low value contrast *No*

Figure 4. Stripes with too much negative space *No*

Figure 5. Curvy stripes are <u>OK</u>.

Figure 6. Too-busy stripes make a less interesting *No*
quilt.

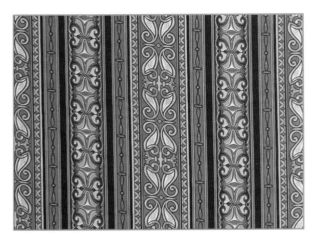

Figure 7. <u>Narrow stripes appropriate for miniatures</u>

Figure 8. Too-wide repeat *No*

Fabrics with very narrow stripes don't work well on full-sized quilts but are great for miniatures (figure 7, page 13)

Some fabrics give the illusion of having stripes but the repeat is so wide it is difficult to distinguish that element of the design (figure 8, page 13).

Shopping for one-fabric quilts is a true adventure for the fabric lover. You will never look at striped fabric in quite the same way again. You will make one surprising quilt after another from these striped fabrics and the results will keep you shopping for more.

Where to Look

Quilters today have many options for shopping for quality fabrics. The quilt shops in your area have the highest quality fabrics. The owners have access to the latest fabric releases that are not usually shown to discount fabric stores.

The discount fabric stores buy fabrics on bolts or flats at reduced prices as they are end runs, printed crookedly on the fabric, or not current releases. The quality may also be compromised by the less than desirable loose weave of the fabrics, which can adversely affect your cutting.

The information age has given quilters the opportunity to go online and shop directly from the manufacturer, other retailers in other parts of the country, or specialty wholesalers. Fabrics shown on the screen can be ordered and received within a couple of days.

When you are vacationing or traveling on business, shop for fabrics that you might not be able to find locally. There are wonderful fabrics available in the most interesting places in the world. A telephone book, the Internet, and local guides are good sources for locating fabric stores in faraway places. The hunt for fabrics is one of the continuing pleasures of quilting.

Getting Set

Preparing the Fabric

Many quilters prefer to prewash their fabric. I do not. I also do not iron the fabric. The fabric is stretched ever so slightly when heat is applied. When working with stripes, it is important to avoid any misalignments that can affect the cutting or sewing.

Your Tool Box

The usual quilter's tools are needed to make one-fabric quilts. You will be working with pieces that may make blocks as large as ten inches. A 15" or even a 20" square ruler will be helpful.

If you don't have a design wall, it's worthwhile to purchase an inexpensive table cover that has a flannel back. It can be tacked to the top of a shelf or door if you have very little wall space. This kind of a substitute design wall is portable and can be taken to class or to your sewing machine to keep the quilt pieces in order. Sew a hem in the bottom and slide in a dowel to help roll it up when not in use. The pieces will remain in place.

A cell phone that takes photos or a digital camera is a great help in keeping track of design ideas.

Determining Size to Cut Squares

The design of a fabric appears over and over again along the yardage. The number of inches between the appearance of a particular motif and the spot where the same motif appears again in the same position on the fabric is the lengthwise repeat of the fabric. There is also a repeat in the design from selvage to selvage. If the design is different all the way across the fabric, then the crosswise repeat is the width of the yardage.

One-fabric quilts are made of triangles that you get by cutting squares twice on the diagonal. The repeat of the fabric design determines the size to cut the squares, which in turn determines the size of blocks you can make with the triangles. The crosswise design repeat is generally smaller than the lengthwise repeat of the design. A rule of thumb is to cut the squares the size of the smaller repeat.

In figure 1, page 16, the floral stripe is 11" wide and the blue stripe print is 3" wide, making the crosswise repeat 14". The lengthwise repeat is 24", so from this fabric you would cut 14" squares. A block made from the triangles cut from the squares would be 12¾" finished.

3"   11"

Figure 1. Striped floral print

Fussy Cuts

Fussy cuts are made by measuring a same-sized square at the same part of the fabric's design each time a square is cut. Both the stripes and the novelty portions of the fabric must be aligned. Notice that the roses on the bottom stripe are the same (figure 2).

Remembering that the lengthwise repeat of the fabric shown in figure 1 is 24", the size of the cut squares (14") is a little more than half of the lengthwise repeat. Fussy-cut squares from this fabric will leave 10" between the end of one cut and the beginning of the next cut. This "wasted" fabric could be used in the borders.

Figure 2. Fussy cut

Random Cuts

Random cuts are made by measuring a same-sized square along a section of fabric, cutting one square right after the other, aligning the stripes but not worrying about the novelty portions of the fabric design.

If you cut the squares randomly, there won't be any wasted fabric between the cuts. Note that while the overall stripes match, the details in them are not the same (figure 3).

Figure 3. Random cut

Where to Cut

Cutting along the edges of a stripe (figure 4) will give a different look to your blocks than if you cut through the center of the stripes (figure 5).

A greater variety in the design is usually achieved by cutting through the center of the stripes.

Figure 4. Cut along the edge of a stripe

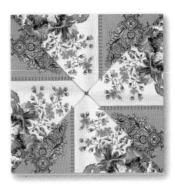

Fig 5. Cut through the center of a stripe

Designing a One-Fabric Quilt

Start by Cutting Squares

The surprising elements of your one-fabric quilt develop as you play with triangles cut from squares. Follow these steps to get started with your one-fabric quilt.

The size of the squares depends on the size of the design repeat in your fabric. A good rule of thumb is to cut your squares the width of the smallest repeat (usually the crosswise repeat but sometimes the lengthwise repeat).

Random or fussy-cut nine squares. (The difference between the two cutting methods is described on page 16.)

The ninth square is a spare for keeping track of the numbering of the triangles and using as a pattern for cutting additional squares.

Play with Four-Triangle Blocks

Layer eight squares face up, oriented the same way, cut them twice on the diagonal, and label the triangles from each square as shown (figure 1).

Select four #1 triangles, arrange them in a square, and place them on a design wall (figure 2).

Figure 1. Cut and labeled square

Figure 2. One block made with four #1 triangles

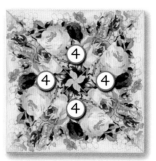

Figure 3. Four four-triangle blocks made with like-numbered triangles

Repeat with the #2 triangles, then the #3 and #4 triangles, so you have four blocks on your design wall. (figure 3).

Try different arrangements of the four blocks to see what patterns develop as they are placed next to one another (figure 4).

Use the remaining 16 triangles and try an eight-block arrangement (figure 5).

Try making some blocks with sets of two different triangles (figure 6).

Then try arranging those blocks (figure 7).

Photograph or record the various arrangements before you rearrange the blocks.

If you like what's happening as the blocks are placed next to each other, cut more squares and expand your design.

Figure 4. Different arrangements of four blocks

Figure 5. Eight-block arrangement

Figure 6. Different triangle arrangements in the blocks

Figure 7. Another eight-block arrangement

Figure 8.

Figure 9. Four-triangle block set on point

Figure 10.

Explore Alternative Designs

If you think your arrangements lack some punch, there are a number of options you can try.

⚱ Cut more squares from a different portion of the fabric.

⚱ Try a different configuration of triangles within the blocks.

⚱ If you fussy cut your squares, try some random-cut squares. If you random cut your original squares, try fussy cutting a set.

⚱ Cut more squares so you can omit one of the numbered sets of triangles. For example, use only the #1, #3, and #4 triangles, eliminating the #2 triangles. (They might be useful later in your border.)

⚱ Try some eight-triangle blocks.

Play with Eight-Triangle Blocks

Cut eight squares and layer them face up, oriented the same way. Cut them twice on the diagonal, and label the triangles from each square as shown (figure 8).

Select four #1 triangles, arrange them in a four-triangle block, set on point, and place them on a design wall (figure 9).

Select four #3 triangles, arrange them in a block, set on point, and place them on the design wall below the four #1 triangles (figure 10).

Make two more blocks with the remaining #1 and #3 triangles and arrange them as shown (figure 11).

Add two #2 triangles to each block as shown (figure 12).

Add two #4 triangles to each square as shown to complete the eight-triangle blocks (figure 13).

Figure 11.

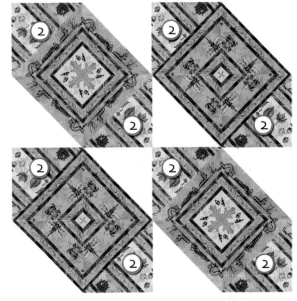

Figure 12.

Take a picture of the design or note the arrangement.

Rearrange the blocks in a different configuration for a different design. Be careful to be consistent with the placement of the triangles within each block, recording the arrangements as you go along.

Try turning the blocks so the #2 triangles form a design in the center (figure 14, page 24).

Try turning the blocks so the #4 triangles form a design in the center (figure 15, page 24).

Try arranging blocks of the #1 and #2 triangles with blocks of the #3 and #4 triangles (figure 16, page 24), then switch the way the triangles are paired (figure 17, page 24).

Continue this process until you are satisfied with your design. Record your final arrangement by photographing it or by using the design worksheet.

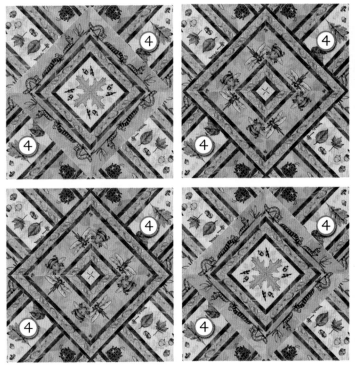

Figure 13.

Figure 14.

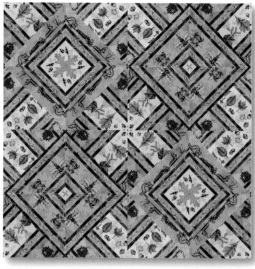

Figure 15.

Figure 16.

Figure 17.

DESIGN TIP

Instead of cutting squares, use a printer. Fold the fabric to an 8"–10" square. Make eight color copies. Layer and cut twice on the diagonal. Use the paper triangles to try out a design (figure 18). Rearrange the pieces to try out different designs. If you're not happy with the designs, refold the fabric and repeat the exercise. Note that your squares of fabric will have to be fussy cut to duplicate any design you create this way.

With only eight squares, you can make a small quilt, wallhanging, or table topper. Simply add a border and you're done (figure 19).

Figure 18. Color-copied squares used to try out an arrangement

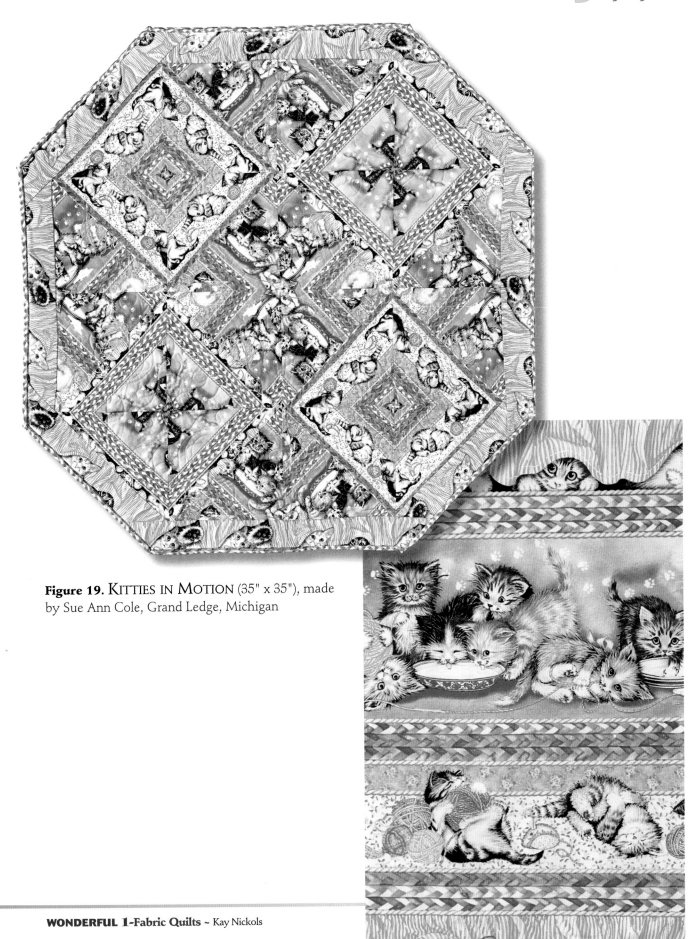

Figure 19. KITTIES IN MOTION (35" x 35"), made by Sue Ann Cole, Grand Ledge, Michigan

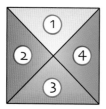

cut 8 squares

Figure 20.

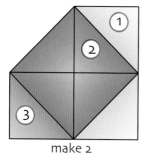

make 2   make 2

Figure 21.

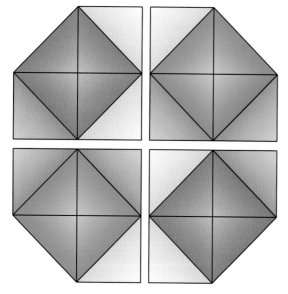

Figure 22.

Figure 23.

Figure 24.

KITTIES IN MOTION is made with the triangles from just eight squares. The clever variation of seven-triangle blocks creates an octagon.

☙ Cut eight squares twice on the diagonal (figure 20).

☙ Make four seven-triangle blocks as shown in figure 21.

☙ Join the four blocks to make the octagon (figure 22).

☙ Add the border, layer, quilt as desired, and bind.

Effects of Different Cuts and Arrangements

Two quilts from the same fabric will look entirely different if the squares are cut from different portions of the fabric's design (figures 23 and 24).

Two quilts from the same fabric will look entirely different if the squares for one are random cut and the squares for the other are fussy cut (figures 25 and 26).

Ready to Go

As you can see, the possibilities are almost limitless. The final look of your one-fabric quilt is affected by all these variations. Where you cut the squares, what size you cut them, whether you decide on four-triangle or eight-triangle blocks, how you arrange the triangles within the blocks—all these affect the final outcome. Maybe you should buy 12 yards of that fabulous striped fabric, just to be sure you'll have enough for all the variations you'll want to try!

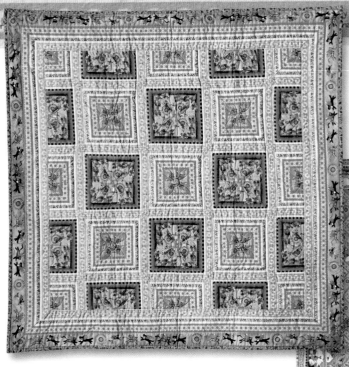

above: **Figure 25.** MAGIC SQUARES, by Jan Gagliano, Haslett, Michigan. Made from squares fussy cut from the same fabric.

right: **Figure 26.** ENCHANTED GARDEN, by Jan Gagliano, Haslett, Michigan. Made from squares random cut from the fabric on this page.

Making a One-Fabric Quilt

When you have determined how you want to cut your squares and which arrangement gives you the most pleasing design, it's time to cut your fabric and sew your quilt.

Cutting the Binding, Borders, and Squares

Cut the selvages from both sides of the fabric.

Cut a 2"–2½" strip from the length of the fabric for your binding.

If you are going to use a no-binding finish or front- or back-fold bindings, you do not need to cut binding strips.

Cut a stripe or stripes the desired width of your borders from the length of your fabric. Be sure to include ¼" seam allowances along both edges. Use the remaining fabric to cut the squares for your quilt (figure 1).

Cut and label all the squares for your quilt. Layer the squares in piles of 4–8 and cut them twice on the diagonal.

Figure 1. Removing selvage and cutting strips for the border and squares

TERRIFIC TIP

Roll the binding and the border strips onto a paper roll to keep them neat (figure 2).

Figure 2. Rolled and ready binding and border strips

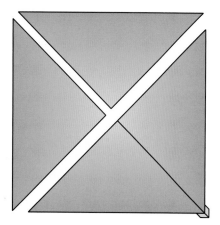

Figure 3. Sewing a four-triangle block

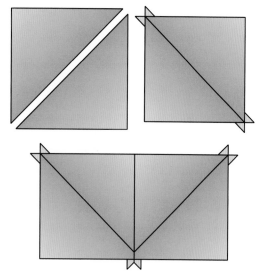

Figure 4. Sewing an eight-triangle block

TERRIFIC TIP

Until you've actually sewn the blocks together, it's never too late to rearrange the blocks for a better design.

Let's Get Sewing!

Arrange the quilt blocks on your design wall.

Rearrange the triangles or blocks if necessary to get the most pleasing design.

Place the pieces of each block on a large ruler or cutting mat to move them to your sewing machine.

Your quilt layout will dictate the way to assemble your quilt.

Sew four-triangle blocks as shown with ¼" seam allowances (figure 3).

Sew eight-triangle blocks as shown with ¼" seam allowances (figure 4).

Be careful not to stretch the bias edges of the triangles as you sew them together.

Finger press seam allowances open as you join the triangles into the blocks.

Trim the "dog ears" from the ends of the triangle seam allowances.

Press all seam allowances open on each completed block with a hot iron.

Return the finished blocks to the design wall, paying careful attention to the orientation of each block.

When all the blocks are sewn, stand back and recheck the layout, making sure each block is in the correct position and oriented correctly in relation to the other blocks.

Join the blocks into rows. Press the seam allowances open.

Join the rows. Press the seam allowances open.

Add the borders.

That's all you need to do to make a fabulous one-fabric quilt.

A NOTE ON PRESSING

Many of my students had never finger pressed nor had they pressed seams open. Some had heard that the seams would be weakened if they were pressed open.

I have found that the seams have a more finished look if the seam allowances are pressed open. An extra advantage is that there is much less bulk to handle at the intersections where eight points come together.

Today's sewing machines have such quality stitching that seams are very tightly sewn and they will not come apart with wear.

TERRIFIC TIP *Ironing*

Use a chopstick, orange stick, or wooden skewer in one hand to open the seams as you heat press.

MARDI GRAS

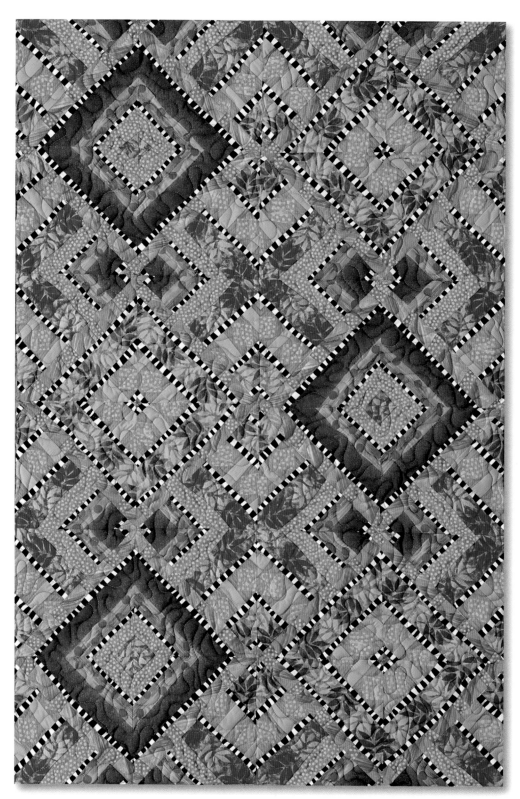

MARDI GRAS, detail, 40" x 59", made by Susan Myers, Haslett, Michigan

This cheerful quilt is like a parade in progress. Using only six eight-triangle blocks makes for a quick project.

⊻ Cut 12 squares twice on the diagonal.

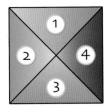

cut 12 squares

⊻ Make three blocks with #1, #2, and #3 triangles.

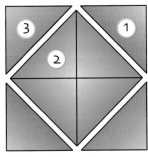

make 3 blocks

⊻ Make three blocks with #1, #3, and #4 triangles

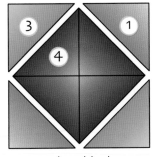

make 3 blocks

⊻ Arrange the blocks in three rows of two blocks each in an alternating pattern.

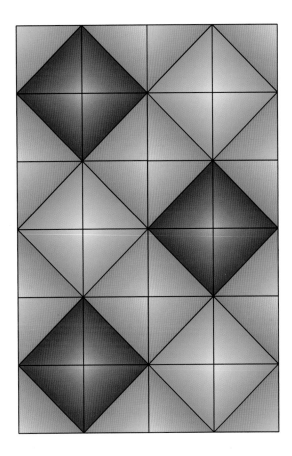

⊻ Join the blocks into rows and join the rows.

⊻ Add the border, layer, quilt as desired, bind, and label your quilt.

African Dancers

AFRICAN DANCERS, 58" x 67", made by Stella Wilcox, Lake Odessa, Michigan

The choice of an African print fabric resulted in this bright, cheerful quilt.

☒ Cut 48 squares twice on the diagonal.

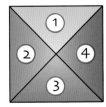

cut 48 squares

☒ Make nine blocks with #1, #2, and #3 triangles.

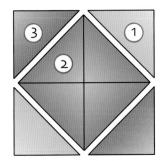

make 9 blocks

☒ Make nine blocks with #1, #3, and #4 triangles.

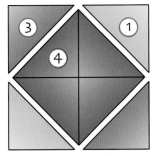

make 9 blocks

☒ Make 6 half-blocks with #1, #2, and #3 triangles.

☒ Make 6 half-blocks with #1, #3, and #4 triangles..

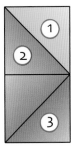
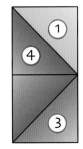

make 6 half-blocks   make 6 half-blocks

☒ Alternate the blocks and half-blocks in an alternating pattern as shown.

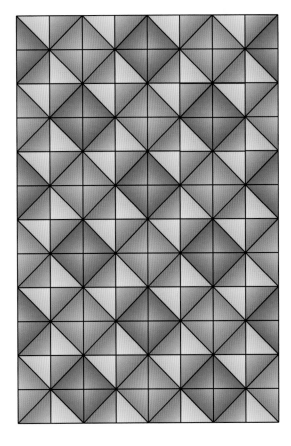

☒ Join the blocks into rows and join the rows.

☒ Add the borders, layer, quilt as desired, bind, and label your quilt.

African Dancers

Sea Garden

SEA GARDEN, 68" x 70", made by Peg Mettler of Haslett, Michigan. Quilted by Susan Meyers, Haslett, Michigan.

The striped fabric in this quilt has many elements in the horizontal design. Peg chose to eliminate a portion of the print before she cut the squares to begin the design process. The rock print stripe was cut so that only the cloud element appeared in the final design. She used eight yards of fabric.

▼ Cut 52 squares twice on the diagonal.

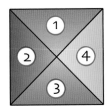

cut 52 squares

▼ Make 13 eight-triangle blocks with the #1, #2, and #3 triangles.

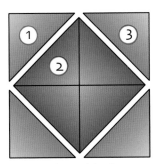

make 13 blocks

▼ Make 12 eight-triangle blocks with the #1, #3, and #4 triangles. (You'll have two #1, two #3, and four # 4 triangles left over.)

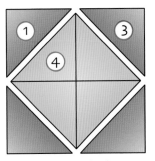

make 12 blocks

▼ Arrange the blocks in an alternating pattern in five rows of five blocks each.

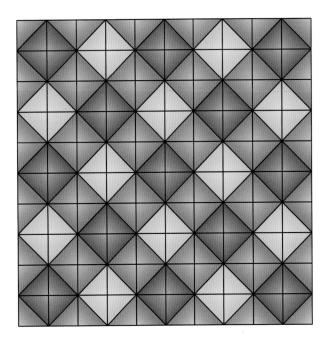

▼ Join the blocks into rows and join the rows.

▼ Add the borders, layer, quilt as desired, bind, and label your quilt.

Sea Garden

Baby Love & Baby Comfort

BABY LOVE, 36" x 48", made by Becky Arambula, Lansing, Michigan

BABY COMFORT, 36" x 48", made by Becky Arambula, Lansing, Michigan

3 yds per quilt

Need two baby quilts in a hurry? Select six yards of a juvenile novelty print and use half the blocks in one quilt and half in the other.

☗ Cut the binding and borders from two different sections of the fabric.

☗ Cut 40 squares twice on the diagonal.

cut 40 squares

☗ Make four-triangle blocks of the like-numbered triangles as shown.

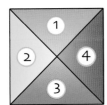
make 10 squares

make 10 squares

make 10 squares

make 10 squares

☗ Arrange the 20 #1 and #2 triangle blocks in a checkerboard pattern for the first quilt.

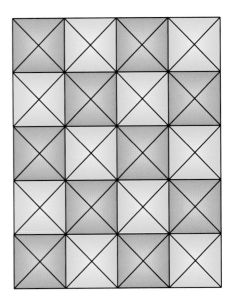

☗ Arrange the remaining 20 blocks in a checkerboard pattern for the second quilt.

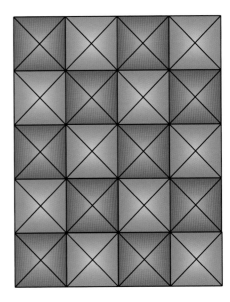

☗ Add the borders, layer, quilt as desired, bind, and label your quilt.

Baby Love & Baby Comfort

Diamonds Aloft

DIAMONDS ALOFT, 66" x 66", made by Phyllis Maxwell, Fowlerville, Michigan.
Quilted by Susan Myers, Haslett, Michigan.

This black floral fabric makes a bold statement. Phyllis used part of a stripe to make the cornerstones in the border.

🔻 Cut 32 squares twice on the diagonal.

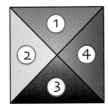

cut 32 squares

🔻 Make 8 eight-triangle blocks with the #1, #2, and #3 triangles.

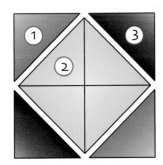

make 8 blocks

🔻 Make 8 eight-triangle blocks with the #1, #3, and #4 triangles.

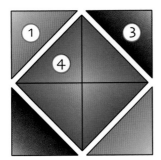

make 8 blocks

🔻 Arrange the blocks in an alternating pattern in four rows of four blocks each.

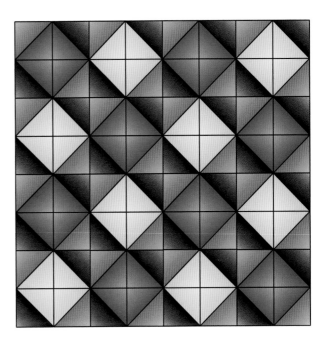

🔻 Add the borders, layer, quilt as desired, bind, and label your quilt.

Diamonds Aloft

Carl's Flower Garden

CARL'S FLOWER GARDEN, 58" x 68", made by Mary Dharamraj, Swartz Creek, Michigan. Quilted by Peter DeLaVergne, Marlette, Michigan.

Mary's quilt was designed from a two-stripe floral. She chose to use the wide floral stripe for the border to expand the openness of the floral design. The quilt was named in honor of her grandfather Carl.

⏷ Randomly cut 32 squares.

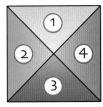

cut 32 squares

⏷ Make the four-triangle blocks of like-numbered triangles as shown.

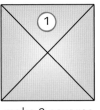

make 8 squares

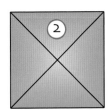

make 8 squares

make 7 squares

make 7 squares

⏷ With the 5 x 7 layout, you'll have some triangles left over. You may want to make blocks with all the triangles so you have more options when doing your final arrangement.

⏷ Arrange the blocks on your design wall, alternating the even-numbered blocks with the odd-numbered blocks. Move them around as needed until you are pleased with the arrangement.

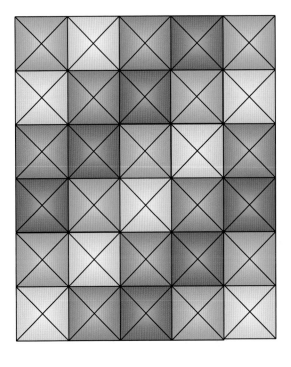

⏷ Join the blocks into rows and join the rows.

⏷ Add the borders, layer, quilt as desired, bind, and label your quilt.

Carl's Flower Garden

One-Fabric Wonder

ONE-FABRIC WONDER, 46" x 67", made by the author. Quilted by
Pat Stinson, Laingsburg, Michigan.

The squares for this quilt were fussy cut. Strips for the border were cut crosswise, from selvage to selvage. Five yards of fabric were used and the border was pieced from the fussy-cut scraps.

✄ Cut 48 squares twice on the diagonal.

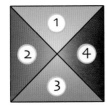

cut 48 squares

✄ Make 12 eight-triangle blocks with the #1, #2, and #3 triangles.

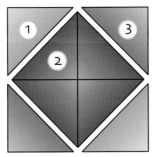

make 12 blocks

✄ Make 12 eight-triangle blocks with the #1, #3, and #4 triangles.

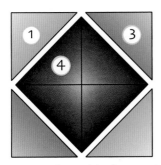

make 12 blocks

✄ Arrange the blocks in an alternating pattern in six rows of four blocks each.

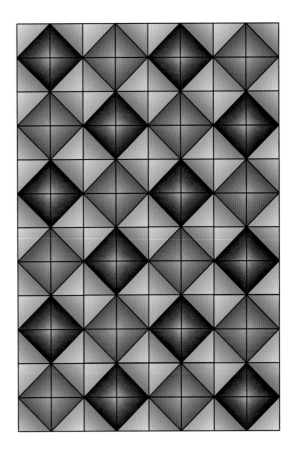

✄ Join the blocks into rows and join the rows.

✄ Add the borders, layer, quilt as desired, bind, and label your quilt.

One-Fabric Wonder

"X" Marks the Spot

"X" MARKS THE SPOT, 52" x 59", made by Amy Reed, Durand, Michigan.
Quilted by Helen Novak, Owosso, Michigan.

It took only (three yards) of fabric to make this lovely quilt. Amy centered the dark stripe of this two-stripe fabric when she cut her squares so there was an equal amount of the light stripe on either side. The result is the bold x's among the roses.

Cut 60 squares twice on the diagonal.

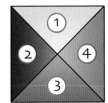

cut 60 squares

Make 15 eight-triangle blocks with the #1 and #2 triangles.

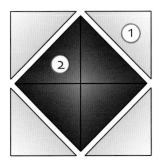

make 15 blocks

Make 15 eight-triangle blocks with the #3 and #4 triangles.

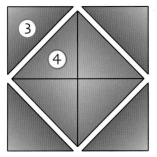

make 15 blocks

Arrange the blocks in an alternating pattern of six rows of five blocks each.

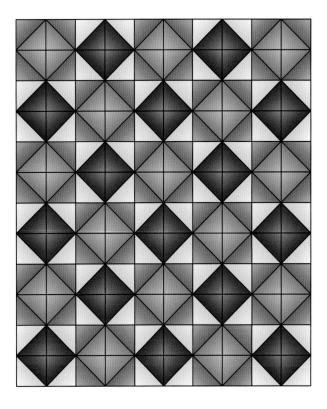

Join the blocks into rows and join the rows.

Add the borders, layer, quilt as desired, bind, and label your quilt.

"X" Marks the Spot

Enchanted Garden

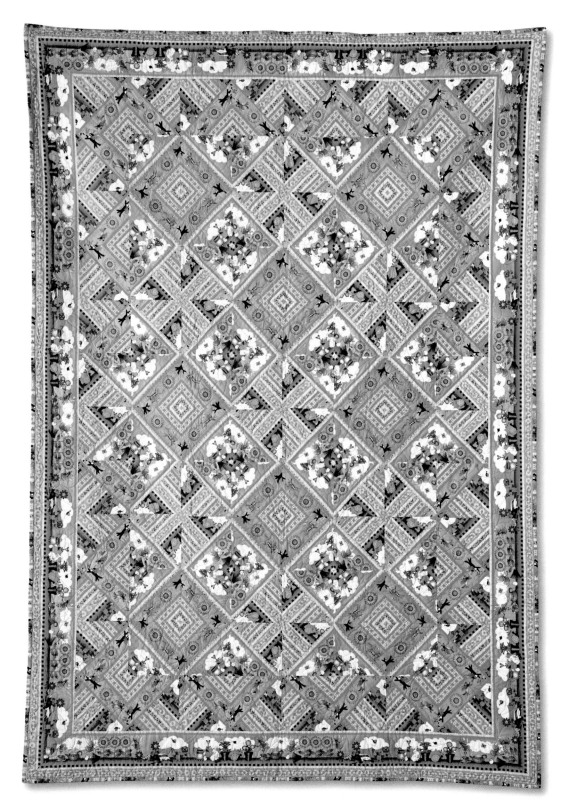

ENCHANTED GARDEN, 58" x 81", made by Jan Gagliano, Haslett, Michigan

The squares in this quilt were randomly cut. The wide border uses a main design stripe that provides a delightful finish to this child's quilt.

☖ Cut 68 squares twice on the diagonal.

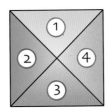

cut 68 squares

☖ Make 8 eight-triangle blocks with #1 and #3 triangles.

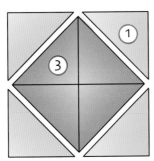

make 8 blocks

☖ Make 7 eight-triangle blocks with #1 and #4 triangles.

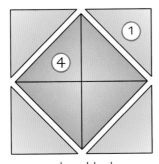

make 7 blocks

☖ Make 12 half blocks as shown with the #2 and #3 triangles.

☖ Make 6 half blocks as shown with the #2 and #3 triangles. (You'll have eight #1, thirty-two

#2, and forty #4 triangles left over—almost enough for another small quilt!)

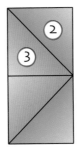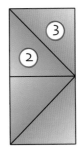

make 12 half-blocks   make 6 half-blocks

☖ Arrange the blocks in five rows of three blocks each. Then position the half blocks around the edges of the quilt as shown so the #2 triangles are along the outer edge.

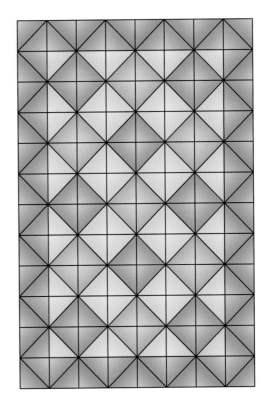

☖ Join the blocks into rows and join the rows.

☖ Add the borders, layer, quilt as desired, bind, and label your quilt.

Enchanted Garden

Blue Roses in Gold

BLUE ROSES IN GOLD, 47" x 47", made by the author. Quilted by Robyn House, Bay City, Michigan.

It took only three yards of this subtle border print to create a wonderfully elegant quilt.

⊻ Fussy cut 20 squares twice on the diagonal.

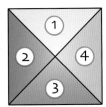

cut 20 squares

⊻ Make five eight-triangle blocks with the #1 and #2 triangles.

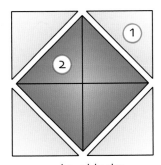

make 5 blocks

⊻ Make four eight-triangle blocks with the #3 and #4 triangles. (You'll have eight triangles left over.)

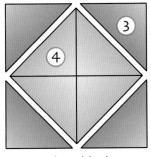

make 4 blocks

⊻ Arrange the blocks in an alternating pattern in three rows of three blocks each.

⊻ Join the blocks into rows and join the rows.

⊻ Add the borders, layer, quilt as desired, bind, and label your quilt.

Blue Roses in Gold

Wonderful Surprise

WONDERFUL SURPRISE, detail, 109" x 124", made by Jean Kaufmann,
Okemos, Michigan. Quilted by Alicia Debello, Lansing, Michigan.

See this king size quilt gracing a bed in the photograph on page 8. Eleven yards of fabric were used with none left over.

⚘ Cut 112 squares twice on the diagonal.

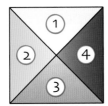

cut 112 squares

⚘ Make 28 eight-triangle blocks with #1, #2, and #3 triangles.

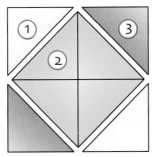

make 28 blocks

⚘ Make 28 eight-triangle blocks with #1, #3, and #4 triangles

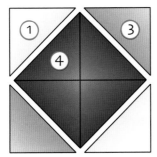

make 28 blocks

⚘ Arrange the blocks in eight rows of seven blocks each in an alternating pattern.

⚘ Join the blocks into rows and join the rows.

⚘ Add the border, layer, quilt as desired, and label your quilt.

Wonderful Surprise

Bed of Roses

BED OF ROSES, 31" x 31", made by Kerrie Nell
Addis, Foxboro, Massachusetts

The free-motion roses in the quilting enhance this floral print throw.

Cut 12 squares twice on the diagonal.

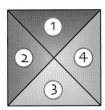

cut 12 squares

Make three four-triangle blocks with #1 triangles.

make 3 squares

Make two four-triangle blocks with #2 triangles. Repeat with #3 and #4 triangles. (You'll have four #2, #3, and #4 triangles left over that you can use to make a table runner.)

make 2 squares

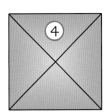

make 2 squares

make 2 squares

Arrange the blocks in three rows of three blocks each in an alternating pattern.

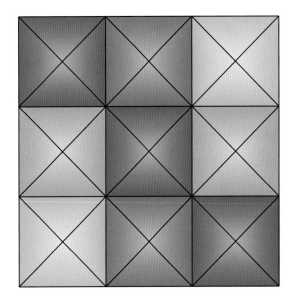

Join the blocks into rows and join the rows.

Add the border, layer, quilt as desired, and label your quilt.

Bed of Roses

Alexander's Ragtime Band

ALEXANDER'S RAGTIME BAND, 66" x 66", made by Linda Baxter Lasco, Paducah, Kentucky. Fabric courtesy of Benartex.

This floral print gives the illusion of a lavishly appliquéd quilt, yet it was done with only six yards of fabulous fabric.

Cut 32 squares twice on the diagonal.

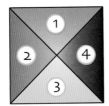

cut 32 squares

Make 8 eight-triangle blocks with the #1, #2, and #3 triangles.

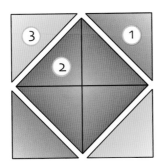

make 8 blocks

Make 8 eight-triangle blocks with the #1, #3, and #4 triangles.

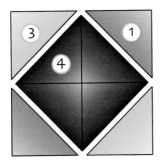

make 8 blocks

Arrange the blocks in an alternating pattern in four rows of four blocks each.

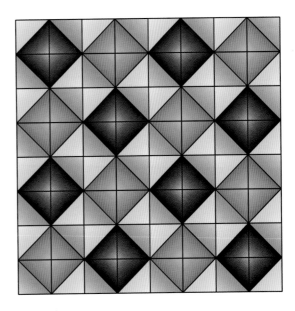

Join the blocks into rows and join the rows.

Add the borders, layer, quilt as desired, bind, and label your quilt.

Alexander's Ragtime Band

Table Runner

TABLE RUNNER, 37" x 13", made by Kerrie Nell Addis, Foxboro, Massachusetts

This runner could be made one block longer without having to cut additional squares.

⛏ Cut 8 squares twice on the diagonal.

 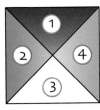

cut 8 squares

⛏ Make two blocks with the #1 triangles.

make 2

⛏ Make one block with the #3 triangles.

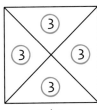

make 1

⛏ Lay out the three blocks on point and position the #2 and #4 triangles as shown.

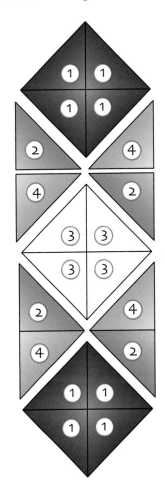

⛏ Sew the #2 and #4 triangles into two-triangle units.

⛏ Join diagonal rows of the two-triangle units and the #1 and #3 blocks.

⛏ Sew the rows together.

⛏ Layer, quilt as desired, and bind the runner.

Table Runner

To Miter or Not to Miter Borders

The stripes are the major design element of one-fabric quilts. These stripes make great borders. They can be mitered, butted, or feature cornerstones. All of these different border treatments help unify the design of the quilt.

Choose a mitered border when you have plenty of fabric and you want to smoothly continue a design around the corners of your quilt. It takes more fabric to miter borders than to butt them (figure 1).

Measure the width and length of the quilt top and add twice the width of the border plus at least another four inches to each measurement to get the length of the border strips you need to cut.

Cut the border strips and add each border to the quilt with a ¼" seam allowance, starting and ending ¼" in from each edge (figure 2). An equal amount of excess border fabric should extend beyond both ends of the quilt.

Figure 1. AFRICAN DANCERS (detail) with mitered borders. Made by Stella Wilcox, Lake Odessa, Michigan.

✄ Lay one corner of the quilt on an ironing surface, right side up. Fold the excess fabric of the two adjacent border pieces back under themselves and line up the folds on a 45-degree angle. Check the angle with the 45-degree line on a rotary-cutting ruler.

✄ Heat press the folds so they meet exactly as you want them to after they are sewn (figure 3).

✄ Place a piece of masking tape over the pressed folds, completely covering the seam line (figure 4).

✄ Turn to the back of the border fabrics, folding the piece of masking tape in half and unfolding the border strips and exposing the pressed seam line.

✄ Sew from the outer edge of the border in toward the quilt top, right along the pressed seam line and against the ridge formed by the folded masking tape. (Be careful not to sew through the tape!) Stop stitching where the two ¼" seams joining the borders to the quilt meet.

✄ Remove the tape and check the seam. Trim the seam allowances to ¼" and press open.

✄ Repeat for the other three corners.

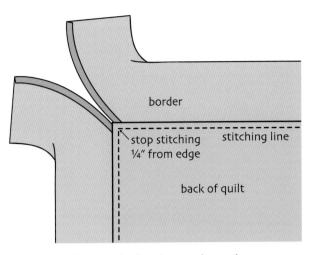

Figure 2. Sewing the borders to the quilt

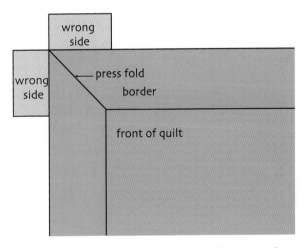

Figure 3. Folding the borders at a 45-degree angle

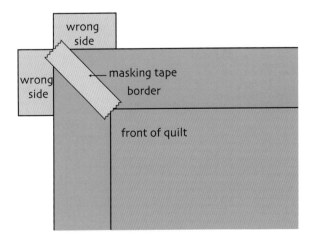

Figure 4. Taping the folds in place

Quilting

An overall quilting pattern is a good choice for a one-fabric quilt so the quilting will not distract from the designs formed by the pieced fabrics. Some quilters like to use invisible thread for the same reason. Others choose variegated thread in colors matching the quilt's fabric so the quilting will blend in, leaving the design elements of the quilt as the main focus.

Be sure to label your quilt. Leftover blocks make great labels. Using a strip of the quilt's fabric for the label is a good way to show how the fabric looked before its transformation into your one-of-a-kind quilt. Labels should always be attached to document the names of the quiltmaker and quilter, the location of each, and the date the quilt was completed. If the quilt is a gift, the name of the recipient and the occasion should be included as well.

About the Author

Kay is known for her enthusiastic teaching methods and for incorporating exotic fabrics into her quilts in unique ways. She is a self-described "shopaholic" and loves to collect fabrics from around the world for the ultimate stash. She incorporates special fabrics into her quilts for both charity and competition.

Kay thrives on being able to teach others the joys of designing one-of-a-kind quilts with one fabric. She also teaches a variety of classes, from beginning quilting to precision piecing. Through the years, she has taken classes with international instructors and has taught as far away as Rabat, Morocco.

Her quilts have been juried into a number of prestigious international quilt shows, exhibited at the Michigan Women's Historical Center, and featured on a *Quilter's Newsletter Magazine* cover.

Ever on the go, Kay is a member of the Capitol City Quilt Guild, the Lansing Area Patchers, the Shiawassee Quilters, the Saginaw Piecemakers, and the Pedal Pushers, a group that meets once a month to bike to nearby quilt shops. She and her husband, Rollie, live in Laingsburg, Michigan.

Other AQS Books

This is only a small selection of the books available from the American Quilter's Society. AQS books are known worldwide for timely topics, clear writing, beautiful color photos, and accurate illustrations and patterns. The following books are available from your local bookseller, quilt shop, or public library.

#7490   us$22.95

#7484   us$22.95

#7489   us$22.95

#7014   us$24.95

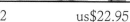

#7492   us$22.95

#7078   us$24.95

#7486   us$19.95

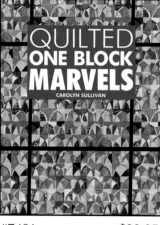

#7491   us$22.95

#5850   us$21.95

Look for these books nationally.
Call or **Visit** our Web site at

1-800-626-5420
www.AmericanQuilter.com